THANI

IMMENSE
SUPPORTING (

We're thrilled you've embarked on this laughter-filled journey with us!

Your thoughts mean the world to us and help other dads (and pun enthusiasts) discover the joy of dad humor. Please take a moment to share your giggles and groans by leaving a review. Just scan the QR code below to do so.

amazon.com/author/serenesquare

WANT EXCLUSIVE FREE GOODIES?

We appreciate your purchase!
Head over to **page 145** to uncover exclusive content as our thank-you gift

Welcome to **"Groan Up Dad Jokes,"** the ultimate collection where humor grows wild and laughter knows no bounds. In this special edition, we've meticulously compiled over 750 of the most hilariously dreadful knee-slappers, head-shakers, and groan-makers known to mankind. But that's not all—we've peppered in a generous serving of snappy one-liners, clever witty quips, and a smorgasbord of whimsically funny made-up situations guaranteed to elicit at least a chuckle, if not a full-on belly laugh.

Whether you're looking to arm yourself with a fresh arsenal of jokes to share at the dinner table, or simply wanting to indulge in some light-hearted reading, this book is your perfect companion. We've poured our hearts and souls into creating a collection that celebrates the dad joke in all its punny glory.

It's our genuine hope that you'll find as much joy in the discovery and delivery of each joke as we did in the curation of this anthology.

SERENE SQUARE PUBLISHING

© Serene Square Publishing, 2023. ALL RIGHTS RESERVED. No part of this book may be used or reproduced in any manner without the prior written permission of the publisher, except in the case of brief quotations embodied in critical reviews and certain other noncommercial uses permitted by copyright law.

This book belongs to:

_____

_____

From _____

_____

My kids told me they want a pony for Christmas.

I normally cook a turkey, but whatever makes them happy!

001

How do you follow Will Smith in the snow?

You follow the fresh prints.

002

How does a priest rinse his salad greens?

Lettuce spray.

003

What do you call a food fight with an unlimited amount of food?

All you can yeet.

004

What did one plate say to the other?

"Dinner's on me."

005

I could make a belt out of these fresh herbs from my garden.

But I won't. because that would be a waiste of thyme.

006

Did you hear the one about the dwarf psychic who'd escaped from prison?

He was a small medium at large.

007

What do you call an Irish person pretending to be Dwayne Johnson?

Shamrock.

008

How do you hide a new video game before Christmas?

You put the cartridge in a pear tree.

009

I sold our vacuum cleaner;

it was just gathering dust.

010

What do you call a lazy baby kangaroo?

Pouch potato.

011

On a sad note, my wife and I have decided we don't want children.

We are going to tell them at dinner tonight.

012

013
Why didn't the cashier get the punch line?

It didn't register.

014
My wife asked me why our fridge was full of stir fry this morning.

Turns out I was sleep wokking again.

015
What does a lawyer wear to court?

A lawsuit.

016
What do turtles on their birthdays.

They shell-abrate.

017
What kind of car does an egg drive?

A beater.

018
Why is there POPcorn but no MOMcorn?

The maize-ogyny runs deep.

It was her first trip to Hawaii and the middle aged lady had noticed that several of her fellow passengers did not pronounce the island name as she had previously assumed it should be pronounced. Anxious not to offend the natives of the island, she decided to approach the first islander she saw and said: "Excuse me, sir, I wonder if you could tell me if it is pronounced Hawaii or Havaii?" "Havaii," the man responded. "Thank you very much," said the grateful tourist. "You're velcome!" said the man.

019

I was listening to some inspirational CDs in the car. They kept telling me to go the extra mile. So I did, and I got lost.

020

Why is ballet nerve wracking?
It keeps you on your toes.

021

Why is it a bad idea to have high rise residential buildings in China?

It's just Wong on so many levels!

Never marry a tennis player,

Love means nothing to them.

What do you call a religious mermaid?

A Mermon.

How do trees get online?

They Log in.

How does the hamburger introduce his girlfriend?

Meat Patty.

Why didn't Chris Rock and Will Smith have turkey for Christmas dinner?

They got beef.

As an aircraft pilot I don't get vaping.
We pilots prefer to take our air plain.

What is Satan's favorite breakfast?
Deviled eggs.

I started learning sign language.
So far, it's been quite handy.

What's better than a talking dog
A spelling bee!

The CEO of IKEA was just elected Prime Minister in Sweden.
He should have his cabinet together by the end of the week.

Algebra doesn't bother me and I tolerate Calculus...
but Graphing is where I draw the line.

My wife asked me if I've seen the dog bowl...

honestly I didn't even know he could!

034

My kid picks up a stone from every hike we go on and on Father's Day each year gives them all to me.

Honestly, it rocks and I appreciate the sediment.

035

A piece of string walks into a bar and orders a drink. The bartender looks at him and says, "We don't serve string here." So, the string goes outside, twists himself up a bit, roughs up his ends, walks back into the bar and orders a drink. The bartender looks at him and says, "Aren't you that little piece of string that was here a few minutes ago?"

The string replies, "I'm a frayed knot."

036

My friend has seasonal allergies and finds the spring blooms a bit overwhelming.

They bring him to his sneeze.

037

If spaghetti and a dead man got into a fight, who would win?

The spaghetti because the dead man pasta way.

038

Did you hear about the thief who got caught stealing a truckload of uranium?

He's currently serving a half-life sentence.

039

How do you get a squirrel to like you?

Just act like you're nuts.

040

Why are frogs always so happy?

They eat whatever bugs them.

041

042

I don't know why people say it's hard to quit smoking.

This is my 7th time quitting this week.

043

What do you call a pile of cats?

A meowntain.

044

Can't wait for the sequel to Dune.

Duly.

045

My Dad always said "time flies like an arrow."

"Fruit flies like a banana."

046

What should you do when you're serving a camel tea?

Ask him if he'd like one hump or two.

047

What's a cat's favorite color?

Purrrrrple.

Little Johnny's kindergarten class was on a field trip to their local police station where they saw pictures, tacked to a bulletin board, of the 10 most wanted criminals. One of the youngsters pointed to a picture and asked if it really was the photo of a wanted person. "Yes," said the policeman. "The detectives want very badly to capture him." Little Johnny asked, "Why didn't you keep him when you took his picture?"

048

A photon walks into a hotel with no luggage and goes to check in. The bellhop asks if he has any bags. The photon replies,

"No sir; I'm travelling light."

049

I went to a meeting where everyone had to say how old they were before we could get started.

We waited for *ages*...

050

So there are two cows eating grass out in the pasture. One cow looks at the other and says, "Hey, have you heard that Mad Cow Disease has been going around lately?"

The other cow looks at him and says, "yeah, thank goodness I'm a penguin!"

051

What did the fisherman say to the magician?

Pick a cod, any cod.

052

Where can you leave your dog while you shop?

In the barking lot.

053

I went to a temporary tattoo parlor to get a tattoo. After it wouldn't wash off the following morning I went back to complain, but...

The tattoo parlor wasn't there...

054

055 — **A duck walks into a drugstore and asks for a tube of lipstick. The cashier says, "That'll be $1.49,"**
and the duck replies, "Just put it on my bill."

056 — **So I got a degree in Egyptology to teach Egyptology to people,**
I think it's a pyramid scheme.

057 — **What happens when you don't pay your exorcist?**
You get repossessed.

058 — **I'm finally upgrading from 1080p to 4K in January.**
It's my new year's resolution.

059 — **If you've seen one big building with a lot of stores inside,**
you've seen the mall.

060

Why can fairies never lie?

Because they always tell the tooth.

061

Do you know why helicopters never fly early in the morning?

Twirly!

062

Every year we rent a bounce house for my son's birthday, but lately the cost has skyrocketed.

It's mostly due to inflation.

063

Why was the computer so tired when it got home from the office?

It had a hard drive.

064

My new sweater I bought for Christmas had a lot of static, so I returned it.

The shop gave me a new one free of charge.

Why can you neither confirm nor deny Santa's existence?

Clausible deniability.

065

What Christmas song is sung at mental hospitals?

Do you hear what I hear…

066

When Bruce became Caitlyn,

did they have a Jenner reveal party?

067

Why did the teacher put rubber bands on her students' heads?

So that they could make snap decisions.

068

My neighbor has a DeLorean.

He drives it from time to time.

069

I bought a dog off a blacksmith today, and as soon as I got home,

it made a bolt for the door.

070

What do you call a Russian cow?

A Mos-cow.

071

What do you call it when a zombie hands you a gift?

A dead give away!

072

What's brown and rhymes with snoop?

Dr Dre.

073

One bird can't make a pun.

But toucan.

074

Why did the cat family move next door to the mouse family?

So they could have the neighbors for dinner.

075

A pun, a play on words, and a limerick walk into a bar.

No joke.

076

077

To the person who wanted me to think the alphabet ends at "T"

I'm onto you.

078

Why won't skeletons fight each other?

They just don't have the guts.

079

How do squid go into battle?

Well-Armed.

080

Do you wanna box for your leftovers?

No, but I'll wrestle you for them.

081

Why don't they play poker in the jungle?

Too many Cheetahs.

082

I only believe in 12.5% of the Bible.

Because I am an eighth-theist.

083

How do you count bovine?

With a cowculator!

084

How does German bread greet each other?

Gluten tag!

085

I attended a wedding the other day were both the bride and groom were Wi-Fi technicians.

I didn't enjoy the ceremony but the reception was great!

086

Just one day ago, we celebrated the first ever holiday dedicated to clowns.

It was jesterday.

087

What's the ocean's most naked fish?

Bare-acuda.

I hate Lyme disease.
It ticks me off.

Why was 4 scared to ask out 5?
Because 4 was 2^2

Why is it spelled "camouflage"
Instead of:

Where do snowmen and snowwomen go to dance?
The snowball.

What do you call the border of South Poland?
A Czechpoint.

My wife wants to split up after I bought the wrong coffee..
I guess it's our grounds for divorce.

My friend wants to become an archaeologist, but I'm trying to put him off.

I'm convinced his life will be in ruins.

094

What do you call Santa when he has no money?

Saint Nickelless.

095

As an infant I wasn't very responsive when my parents played peek-a-boo.

So they admitted me to the ICU.

096

Karl Marx is a historically famous philosopher but no-one ever mentions his sister,

Onya, the inventor of the starting pistol.

097

I used to teach origami.

But there was too much paperwork.

098

099

I'm never asking a Swiss person to write a cheesy story again.

It was full of holes.

100

What do you call a donkey with only three legs?

A wonkey!

101

Which U.S. state is famous for its extra-small soft drinks?

Minnesota!

102

A turtle is crossing the road when he's mugged by two sloths. When the police ask him what happened, the shaken turtle replies,

"I don't know. It all happened so fast."

103

I was playing chess yesterday, and the opponent started to yell at me.

He kept losing his piece with every move.

Did you hear about the racing snail who got rid of his shell? He thought it would make him faster,

but it just made him sluggish.

(104)

What language does a magician speak?

Vanish.

(105)

Only two years ago, my wife's gynecologist delivered pizza.

To this day, they both think it's a bad name.

(106)

I gave up my seat to a blind person on the bus.

That's how I lost my job as a bus driver.

(107)

What do you call birds that stick together?

Velcrows!

(108)

109. I am terrified of elevators
so I am taking steps to avoid them.

110. Why do treehouses make good businesses?
They typically have good branch managers.

111. I thought I was alone in the cemetery,
but then I heard somebody coffin.

112. A guy made the mistake of bringing his attack dog to the circus.
As might have been expected, it went straight for the juggler.

113. A slice of apple pie is $2.50 in Jamaica and $3.00 in the Bahamas.
These are the pie rates of the Caribbean.

114 · Did you hear the one about the kid who started a business tying shoelaces on the playground?

It was a knot-for-profit.

115 · What do you call a disease you get in an airport?

The flew.

116 · I'm reading a horror story in braille. Something bad is going to happen,

I can just feel it.

117 · How did the hacker get away from the police?

He ransomware.

118 · How many paranoids does it take to change a light bulb?

Who wants to know?

119. My friend had a triple bypass surgery appointement yesterday but he didn't go.

He had a change of heart at the last minute.

120. What comes after man?

Postman.

121. What would you call somebody who travels from Budapest to Istanbul?

Hungary for Turkey.

122. What did the DNA say to the other DNA?

"Do these genes make me look fat?"

123. What do you call a dinosaur who's hiding from the cops?

Doyouthinkhesaurus.

124. As a joke, I hid the arms of the dummy skeleton in the bio lab.

My teacher was not amused.
He did not find that humerus.

125. Where do fish go to work?

The ofish.

126. I just found out that there is no training for garbage men.

They just pick things up as they go along.

127. Last night my wife told me it's over and walked out.

I always wait until the end of the credits before I leave the theater.

128. Elon Musk is originally from South Africa

Which is weird, you think he'd be from mad-at-gas-car.

129. How does a bee get to school?"

The buzz.

130. What do you call a crocodile that suffers from kleptomania?

A crookodile.

131. My friend went missing in a horse barn.

We suspect foal play.

132. Did you hear about the missing Zamboni driver?

He has yet to resurface.

133. What's the best day to fly a kite?

Windsday.

134. Did you hear about the two bedbugs that fell in love?

They're getting married in the spring.

What did the tailor say after his client fired him?

"Suit yourself."

Why was the comedian accused of assaulting her audience?

She gagged them and left them in stitches.

Why couldn't the cops catch the wallpaper thief?

There was a big cover-up.

Why was the firefighter lovesick?

She couldn't get over an old flame.

How does the man on the moon cut his hair?

Eclipse it.

A cheeseburger walks into a bar.

The bartender says, "Sorry, we don't serve food here."

141. Bruce Lee was fast, but have you ever heard of his even faster brother?

Sudden Lee.

142. Where did the vampire open his savings account?

At the blood bank.

143. Why did the elephant go running?

It wanted to jog its memory.

144. What's a chicken's favorite composer?

Bach.

145. What kind of TV do you find in a haunted house?

A big-scream TV.

146. What is a bug's favorite sport?

Cricket.

147. What did the tomato say to the other tomato during a race?
Ketchup.

148. What kind of music do planets like?
Neptunes.

149. I recently paid $1 for a wig.
It was a small price toupee.

150. I slept like a log last night.
Woke up in the fireplace!

151. Did you hear about the claustrophobic astronaut?
He just wanted a little more space.

152. Son: I'll call you later.
Dad: Don't call me later, call me Dad!

153

What do you call a fish wearing a bowtie?

Sofishticated.

154

We all know about Murphy's Law: anything that can go wrong will go wrong. But have you heard of Cole's Law?

It's thinly sliced cabbage.

155

Why do cows wear bells?

Because their horns don't work.

156

I am on a sea food diet.

I see food and I eat it.

157

Why didn't the police catch the woman who robbed the Laundromat?

She made a clean getaway.

158. The eyelash and the lipstick were in a fight.

But don't worry, they'll make up.

159. Someone was throwing Stephen King books at everyone in the library and I couldn't figure out what was going on.

But then it hit me.

160. What is it called when a cow spies on you?

A steak out.

161. To whoever entered our bar just to steal the limbo sticks,

how low can you go?

162. What do you call the offspring of two dump-trucks?

Dumplings.

What do you call someone who's allergic to burnt bread?

Black-toast intolerant.

163

What happens when the number of bullies at school goes up?

The mean increases.

164

What type of music should you listen to while fishing?

Something catchy.

165

Why shouldn't you write with a broken pencil?

Because it's pointless.

166

What kind of underwear do lawyers wear?

Briefs!

167

Do I enjoy making court house puns?

Guilty.

168

What do you call it when people accuse Johnny Depp without listening his side?

Heard mentality

169

How often should you tell a joke to a scientist?

Periodically.

170

What do you call zombies living together?

Tomb mates.

171

I'm starting to feel bad for my coffee.

Poor guy gets mugged everyday.

172

What did the janitor say when he jumped out of the closet?

Supplies!

173

How do baby birds know how to fly?

They just wing it.

What do you call a fish's date?

His gill-friend.

My wife always tells me that I'm too indecisive...

I'm not sure how to feel about it.

Why do pirates never take a bath before they walk the plank?

Because they always wash up on shore.

Do you know why we're so used to using shampoo?

Conditioning.

Where do I keep all my dad jokes?

In a DAD-abase.

Want to hear a joke about construction?

I'm still working on it!

180

I've been thinking about taking up meditation.

I figure it's better than sitting around doing nothing.

181

What do you call a mom who turns into a dad?

Transparent.

182

Why do astronauts use Linux?

Because you can't open windows in space.

183

A lion once ate an optimistic person.

Sadly, he was only half full!

184

Why did the keyboard get fired?

He was missing a shift.

185

186. When should you bring your father to class?

When you have a pop quiz.

187. What did one elevator say to the other?

I think I'm coming down with something!

188. How do you catch a whole school of fish?

With bookworms.

189. What do houses wear?

Address.

190. Why do pregnant cows have so much energy?

They're heavily calfinated.

191. Why did the duck become a spy?

He was good at quacking codes.

I heard that Neil Armstrong reacted very emotionally to being picked for Apolo 11.

He was over the moon.

192

Why do balding men go to the bathroom so frequently?

Toupee.

193

Thank you, student loan, for helping me through college.

I don't think I can ever repay you.

194

Why won't banks allow kangaroos to open accounts?

Their checks always bounce.

195

If sweet dreams are made of cheese,

Who am I to dis-a-brie?

196

197. Why is a jellyfish so sad?

Because there's no peanut butter fish.

198. What do you get when a chicken lays eggs on top of a hill?

Eggrolls.

199. Do history teachers ever marry?

No, they just get dated.

200. Why did George Washington chop down the cherry tree?

I'm stumped.

201. What should you do when someone throws a goose at you?

Duck.

202. What do they call James Bond taking a bath?

Bubble-O-Seven.

203

Which bird is always out of breath?

The puffin.

204

I built a model of Mount Everest and my son asked if it was to scale.

"No," I said. "It's to look at."

205

What do you call a zombie who writes music?

A decomposer.

206

What did the scarf say to the hat?

"You go on a-head, I'll go around."

207

My boss asked me why I only get sick on work days.

I said it must be my weekend immune system.

208

How much does a chimney cost?

It's free. It's on the house.

209. **85% of Americans don't know how to do basic math.**

Thank God I'm part of the other 25%.

210. **I applied for a job hanging mirrors.**

It's something I can see myself doing.

211. **I walked into a bar and noticed that their dartboard was on the ceiling.**

It made me throw up.

212. **Did you know that Stephen King has a son named Joe?**

I'm not *joking*, but he is.

213. **Every morning at the breakfast table, I tell my kids I'm going for a jog, but then I don't.**

It's a running joke.

An admiral is staring off the deck of his battleship at the approaching enemy on the horizon. "Fetch my red shirt," the admiral says to his first officer. "If I'm wounded in battle, I don't want the men to see I'm bleeding. It will kill morale." "But sir," says the first officer, "there is a fleet of fifteen ships coming right for us."

"Oh," the admiral sighs. "Well, in that case go grab my brown pants."

214

My sister came out today, and told us that she identifies as a musical instrument.

I always had my suspicions about our Monica.

215

Why is the dragon considered to be the best rapper?

It always spits fire.

216

Why do English people pronounce it as Bri'ish?

Because they drank the T.

The other night I was laying in bed looking at the stars and thinking.

Where the hell is my roof?

What do you call a factory that makes okay products?

A satisfactory.

How would you describe one ply toilet paper?

Tearible.

If you suck at playing trumpet,

that's probably why.

My dog is a genius. I asked him "What's two minus two?"

He said nothing.

223 **My wife left me because of my gambling addiction.**
But I know I can win her back.

224 **My friend let me borrow her audiobook, but I lost it.**
Now I'll never hear the end of it.

225 **I argued with the cashier my bill was $7.23 and not $723.**
He didn't get the point.

226 **My wife asked me to put ketchup on the shopping list.**
Now I can't read anything.

227 **My dad made a lot of money off of his famous song about the number four. When he passed away, he left its rights to me.**
I am the heir to his four tune.

228. I just found out my toaster isn't waterproof!

It shocked me.

229. What is Homer Simpsons favorite ice cream?

Cookie D'OH!

230. Who is Superman's most religious enemy?

Lex Lutheran.

231. Where do lettuces practice law?

At the salad bar.

232. Did you hear the one about the vampire?

It was a vein attempt at humor.

233. Pun walked into a room and killed 10 people

Pun in, ten dead.

Why couldn't the sailors play cards?

Because they were standing on the deck!

234

What did the dentist name his boat?

The Tooth Ferry.

235

Why did the teacher wear dark glasses?

Because her class was so bright.

236

What do celebrity vampires receive?

Fang mail.

237

What do you get when you cross a witch with ice?

A cold spell.

238

My wife gets made when I mess with her red wine.

So I added fruit and lemonade to it.
Now she sangria than ever!

239

240. Why do dogs float in water?

Because they are good buoys.

241. Why did the stadium get so hot after the game?

Because all the fans left.

242. The guy who stole my diary died yesterday.

My thoughts are with his family.

243. I can sum up 2024 in one word.

Eight.

244. Where do terrorists go when they die?

Everywhere.

245. What do you call a typo on a headstone?

A grave mistake.

246. I named my dog "5 miles."

So that I could frequently say,
"I walked 5 miles today."

247. How was Rome split in two?

With a pair of Caesars.

248. I used to hate facial hair

but then it grew on me.

249. I'll never tell my accountant a joke again.

He just depreciates them.

250. Did you know that regardless of age, gender or physical size, everyone's bones weigh exactly the same?

1 skele-ton.

251

How many tickles does it take for an octopus to laugh?

Ten-tickles.

252

My friend told me he eats potatoes at breakfast every morning.

That's one way to starch your day.

253

I always wanted to be a doctor.

But I never had the patience.

254

Why did the athlete take up bowling?

She thought it would be up her alley.

255

I got my wife a prosthetic leg for Christmas

It wasn't her main present, just a stocking filler.

256

My friend and I are fighting over a golf club.

It's driving a wedge between us.

257. Did you hear about the French general who stepped on a landmine?

Napoleon Blown Apart.

258. What did one hat say to the other

Stay here! I'm going on ahead.

259. What do farmers plant in their sofas?

Couch potatoes.

260. Why did the mama bread get mad at her kids?

They were always loafing around.

261. Why couldn't the pepper practice archery?

Because it didn't habanero

262. When you're a kid, you know the name every dinosaur.

When you're an adult you only know one...
My-body-saur

263. Why do balloons hate Ed Sheeran concerts?

They are afraid of pop music.

264. I accidentally sprayed deodorant in my mouth.

Now when I speak, I have an Axe scent.

265. My friend told me I don't understand how irony works.

Which is ironic, because we were at a bus stop.

266. The earth is 70% water and uncarbonated.

Which technically makes the earth flat.

267. What gets Jackie Chan sick every winter?

Kung flu.

268. How did the fisherman go deaf?

He lost his herring.

269. What do you call a king's sore throat?

A royal pain in the neck.

270. Which branch of the military accepts toddlers?

The infantry.

271. Why don't seagulls fly over the bay?

Because then they'd be bagels.

272. Two trees met on tinder,

They are now kindling a romance.

273. What's the best time to go to the dentist?

Tooth-hurty.

274. What kind of tea is hard to swallow?

Reality.

275. Why don't you buy things with Velcro?

It's a rip-off.

276. If you slap Dwayne Johnson's butt

You officially hit rock bottom.

277. What do you call a duck that's addicted?

A quackhead.

278. How did the barber win the race?

He knew a shortcut.

279. What is the fastest growing city in the world?

Capital of Ireland. It's Dublin every day.

280. I think my wife is putting glue on my antique weapons collection.

She denies it but I'm sticking to my guns!

281.

What should we do with a dead chemist?

Barium.

282.

I ate a Pb & jelly sandwich.

Wouldn't recommend, now I've got lead poisoning.

283.

Cooking out this weekend?

Don't forget the pickle. It's kind of a big dill.

284.

A woman is on trial for beating her husband to death with his guitar collection. The judge asks her,

"First offender?" She says,
"No, first a Gibson! Then a Fender!"

285.

What did one cannibal say to the other while they were eating a clown?

"Does this taste funny to you?"

286. Justice is a dish best served cold.

If it were served warm, it would be justwater.

287. What did the ocean say to the beach?

Nothing, it just waved.

288. I gave away all my batteries today.

Free of charge.

289. The world tongue-twister champion just got arrested.

I hear they're gonna give him a really tough sentence.

290. There used to be a bee hive in a church. One day, suddenly they all left.

It was a bunch of bee-leavers.

291

Where do pancakes rise?

In the yeast.

292

My new girlfriend works at the zoo

I think she's a keeper.

293

Why are waiters one of the best employees?

Because they bring a lot to the table.

294

What did one wall say to the other?

"Meet me at the corner."

295

Why did Bobby tie a clock to his palms?

He wanted to have time on his hands.

296

Why did the computer cross the road?

To get a byte to eat.

297

What did the milkmaid say to the anxious butter?

"You'll have to wait your churn."

298

Why do cows have hooves instead of feet?

Because they lactose.

299

I lost my wife 2 years ago today.

She's brilliant at hide and seek.

300

What's a ninja's favorite type of shoes?

Sneakers!

301

Not sure if you have noticed, but I love bad puns.

That's just how eye roll.

302

Why did the orange lose the race?

It ran out of juice.

303. My wife bet me $1000 I couldn't turn spaghetti into a car.

You should have seen her face when I drove pasta.

304. What concert costs just 45 cents?

50 Cent featuring Nickelback!

305. What do you call someone who pretends to be Swedish?

An artificial Swedener.

306. My friend was bragging that his 3D printer can print a gun but I wasn't impressed.

I had a Canon printer for years.

307. My friend is addicted to drinking brake fluid, but tells me not to worry about him.

He can stop any time.

308. How do you get a tissue to dance?
Put a little boogey in it.

309. Why don't eggs make good quarterbacks?
When their defense cracks, they're too quick to scramble.

310. What did the plugged-in phone get arrested for?
It was charged for battery.

311. What do you get when you cross a detective with an alligator?
An investi-gator.

312. What do you call an angle that's gotten into a car crash?
A rectangle.

313. What did the alien say to the pop bottle

"Take me to your liter."

314. What do you get when you mix a fish and an elephant?

Swimming trunks.

315. What is Snow White's brother's name?

Egg White. And that's no yoke!

316. Why didn't the police arrest the runner?

She had a good track record.

317. Why did the student put on eyeliner and mascara in school?

Because the teacher said she was giving the class a makeup exam.

318

Does a roller coaster like its work?

It has its ups and downs.

319

I asked my date to meet me at the gym but she never showed up.

I guess the two of us aren't going to work out.

320

Do you know how to make gold soup?

Just put 24 carrots in it!

321

I tried to work at a knife factory.

But I just wasn't cut out for the job.

322

My next door neighbor and I became good friends, so we decided to share our water supply.

We got a long well.

323. **Did you know that Milk is the fastest liquid on earth?**

It's pasteurized before you even see it.

324. **I saw an ad that read: "TV for sale, $1, volume stuck on full."**

I thought to myself, "I can't turn that down!"

325. **Why did the cucumber need a lawyer?**

It was in a pickle.

326. **Within minutes, the detectives knew what the murder weapon was.**

It was a brief case.

327. **After an unsuccessful harvest, why did the farmer decide to try a career in music?**

Because he had a ton of sick beets.

328. Why did the comedian put on his sneakers?

He wanted to tell a running joke.

329. Why did the cellphone wear his glasses?

Because he lost his contacts.

330. I learned today that you cannot be whoever you want to be.

Turns out Identity theft is a crime.

331. Did you hear about the bacon cheeseburger who couldn't stop telling jokes?

It was on a roll.

332. I was just reminiscing about the beautiful herb garden I had when I was growing up.

Good thymes.

333

My wife told me I had to stop acting like a flamingo.

So I had to put my foot down!

334

What do you get when you cross a cow with an earthquake?

Milkshakes.

335

How does the snake charmer sign his letters?

"Love and hisses."

336

Why did the police officers arrest the python after the accident?

It was a hiss and run.

337

What accidents happen every 24 hours?

Day breaks and night falls.

338

Why was there no food left after the Halloween party?

Because everyone was goblin.

339. Why did the boy quit his job at the eraser factory?

His work rubbed him the wrong way.

340. What kind of shoes does a lazy person wear?

Loafers.

341. Why was the broom late for work?

It over-swept.

342. An apple a day keeps the doctor away

if thrown hard enough.

343. How can you tell it's a dogwood tree?

By the bark.

344. What do you call someone who makes dad jokes but has no kids

a faux pa!

345
Apple just announced their next groundbreaking product.

The iShovel

346
What lights up a soccer stadium?

A soccer **match**.

347
What do you call a shoe made of a banana?

A slipper!

348
I was kidnapped by mimes once.

They did unspeakable things to me.

349
What's the difference between a poorly dressed man on a unicycle and a well-dressed man on a bicycle

Attire.

350. What kind of music did the pilgrims listen to?

Plymouth rock.

351. I work in a kitchen, and the other day I was thinking of stealing a mixing utensil.

I might get fired, but it's a whisk I'm willing to take.

352. Why did the Martian leave the Mars party?

He didn't like the atmosphere.

353. What did the owner of the coffee shop give to her new employees?

A list of do's and donuts.

354. What do you call a snake that works for the Government?

A Civil Serpent.

355. How do you think the unthinkable?

With an itheberg.

356. What do you call a Christian fruit?

A peacher.

357. Why did the stuttering prisoner die?

He couldn't finish his sentence.

358. What do mountain goats use to hang their clothes.

A cliffhanger.

359. What do you call a person who puts poison in someone's corn flakes?

A cereal killer.

Why is it good to tell ghost stories in hot weather?

Because they are so chilling.

360

What would you get if you crossed a dinosaur with a pig?

Jurassic Pork.

361

An old guy in his car is driving home from work when his wife rings him on his car phone. "Honey", she says in a worried voice, "be careful. There was a bit on the news just now, some lunatic is driving the wrong way down the freeway".

"It's worse than that", he replies, "there are hundreds of them!"

362

My dog ate a string of christmas lights. Thankfully, the vet was able to remove them.

He said my dog was delighted!

363

What's worse than finding a worm in the apple you're eating?

Finding half a worm!

364

Why did the Mexican man push his wife off a cliff?

Tequila.

365

Did you hear about the locksmith who is also a musician?

He recently wrote a song which has a lovely key change.

366

If Snoop Dogg were an actual dog, what breed would he be?

Labradizzle.

367

What do you get when you cross a porcupine with a baby goat?

One stuck-up kid!

368

What did the mother kangaroo say when her baby was kidnapped?

"Somebody help me catch that pickpocket!"

369

I heard Will Smith's wife is about to divorce him.

It's Hair loss.

370

I told my dad a joke about the creator of The Simpsons.

He's Groening.

371

I told my son that Humpty Dumpty is going to have a terrible summer but not to worry because I'm sure...

he'll have a great fall!

372

A freeway, an autobahn and a bike lane walk into a bar in a bad part of town. As they are enjoying their drinks, a couple of tough guys walk up and try to pick a fight with autobahn because of his accent. Bike lane steps out from behind freeway and fixes them with an icy glare. They apologize and leave the bar. Freeway whispers to the barman, "What was that all about?" "Don't you know?" Replies the barman, "He's a freaking cycle path!"

373

Why aren't koala bears considered real bears?

Because they never get the koalafications.

374

6:30 is the best time on a clock.

Hands down.

375

There are two rules in life.

i) Never tell anyone everything.

376

Did you hear that the fire-eater got engaged?

He ran into an old flame.

377

Which movie director always forgets to wear sunblock?

Steven Peelberg.

378

What kind of car does an egg drive.

Yolkswagen.

379

A mom walks into a store and asks if she could have a toy tractor for her daughter.

The store clerk replies, "I'm sorry, ma'am, but we don't do exchanges."

My wife asked for me to hand her her lipstick. I accidentally passed her a glue stick. She's still not talking to me.

How do you organize a space party?

You planet.

What do turtles on their birthdays.

They **Head out** for a party.

A girl named IKEA had to change her name...

They kept setting her up for jokes.

385

How does a programmer lose his mind?

Bit by bit.

386

I've got a phobia of over-engineered buildings

It's a complex complex complex.

387

Why doesn't James Bond fart in bed?

Because it will blow his cover!

388

Why are there pop tarts but no mom tarts.

Because of the pastry-archy.

389

Where does a pirate keep his buccaneers?

On his buccan head.

390

I just saw a hipster wearing two monocles, one on each eye.

He made a spectacle of himself.

391

Helvetica and Times New Roman walk into a bar. "Get out of here!" shouts the bartender, "we don't serve your type."

392

I have a pencil that used to belong to Shakespeare, but he chewed on it a lot.

I can't even tell if it's 2B or not 2B.

393

The only thing Flat-Earthers have to fear...

Is sphere itself!

394

Why did the Cyclops have to shut down his school?

He only had one pupil.

395

How did the Trump supporter fall off his motorcycle?

He was leaning too far to the right.

396. My Cat is LGBTQ+ only at meal times

That's the only time she comes out of the closet.

397. What is invisible and makes clucking sounds?

A poultry-geist!

398. Why does the Giraffe have such a long neck?

Because it's head is so far away!

399. What did the evil chicken lay?

Deviled eggs.

400. You can't blame anyone else if you fall in your driveway.

That's your own asphalt.

401. I put a bunch of fake fish in the neighborhood pond

They're De Kois.

402 — Why are sheep anxious at night?

Because so many people are counting on them.

403 — What can you do if you have too much cake?

You can halve your cake and eat in two.

404 — My wife and I wear the same size shoe.

We're sole mates.

405 — Dog ownership is more expensive than you think.

There's a lot of hidden fleas.

406 — What did Mr. Volcano say to Mrs. Volcano?

I lava you.

407 — Why did the non-binary prospector head west?

There was gold in them/their hills!

408. The final four letters in the word "queue" aren't silent...

They're just waiting their turn.

409. When does a joke become a dad joke?

When it's full groan!

410. The past, present, and future walk into a bar.

It was tense.

411. Which is faster, hot or cold?

Hot, because you can catch cold.

412. I got a reversible jacket for Christmas,

I can't wait to see how it turns out.

413. The other day a clown held the door open for me.

It was a nice jester.

My kids asked me what "opaque" means.

I said, "according to the dictionary, it's still unclear."

414

Why don't eggs tell jokes?

They'd crack each other up.

415

Steve Jobs would have made a better president than Donald Trump.

But that's comparing apples to oranges.

416

SpongeBob may be the main character of the show.

But Patrick is the star.

417

Why can't you send a duck to space?

Because the bill would be astronomical.

418

No matter how much you push the envelope,

it's still stationery.

419

How do pirates know they're pirates?

They think, therefore they ARRRRRRRgh!

420

What do you get when you cross a dinosaur with a firework?

Dino-mite.

421

What do you call a dentist who doesn't like tea?

Denis.

422

A grasshopper walks into a bar. The bartender looks at him and says, "Hey, they named a drink after you!

"Really?" replies the grasshopper. "There's a drink named Stan?"

423

Do you know why the French only eat one egg for breakfast?

Because in France, one egg is un ouef.

424

425

Where do baby calves go for lunch?

The calf-eteria.

426

Why wouldn't the pet store take back the chimp?

They didn't offer a monkey-back guarantee.

427

Why did the football coach go to the bank?

To get his quarter back.

428

What's the opposite of artificial intelligence?

Natural stupidity.

429

What does the chicken see?

The chicken Caesar salad.

430

You know what happens when clowns fart?

Smells funny.

431. A boy asks his father for a spider for his birthday. The father stops by the pet shop on the way home from work to find out more about spiders. "What does one of those big ones cost?" the father asks, pointing into the glass case full of the arachnids. "About fifty dollars," the store clerk replies. "Fifty dollars!" the father replies. "I'll just find a cheap one off the web."

432. **What do you call a priest who becomes a lawyer?**
A father in law.

433. **Why did the scarecrow get an award?**
He was outstanding in his field.

434. **What happens to Jason Momoa once he dies?**
He becomes Jason Nomoa.

A Roman cannibal was sent to compete in the colosseum as punishment for killing and eating his wife. You'd think he had regrets...

but he was gladiator.

435

The local police must be color blind. Someone stole all of my blue paint. I reported it, and I got a call saying...

they caught the thief red-handed.

436

What's Whitney Houston's favorite type of coordination?

"Hand eeeeyeeeee......"

437

What do you call a fake noodle?

An impasta.

438

My wife went to the doctor to deliver our baby.

I keep trying to tell her that babies need their livers.

439

Where does Darth Vader get his coffee

DeathStarBucks.

440

Which laptop can sing?

A-Dell.

441

What do cows most like to read?

Cattle-logs.

442

What's Forrest Gump's password?

1forrest1

443

What did the cake say to the frosting on Valentine's Day?

"Without you I'd be muffin."

444

Nurse: "Blood type?"

Dad: "Red, usually wet"

445

(WARNING 18+)

19

446

Did you hear about the guy who froze to death at the drive-in?

He went to see Closed for the Winter.

447

A cheese factory exploded in France.

Da brie was everywhere!

448

A vowel saves another vowel's life.

The other vowel says, "Aye E! I owe you!"

449

I refused to believe my road worker father was stealing from his job...

But when I got home all the signs were there.

450

My wife told me to stop singing Wonderwall.

I said maybeee.

451

452 **What do you call a beehive without an exit?**

UnBeeLeaveable!

453 **To the person who stole my place in the queue.**

I'm after you now.

454 **Why are skeletons so calm?**

Because nothing gets under their skin.

455 **A Mexican magician started counting "uno....dos..."**

then, poof, he disappeared...without a tres!

456 **I managed to get B's in all my classes.**

You should have seen the expression on the face of my teacher and fellow students when they got swarmed.

457. Stop looking for the perfect match.
Use a lighter.

458. I ordered a chicken and an egg from Amazon.
I'll let you know.

459. We all know where the Big Apple is,
but does anyone know where the Minneapolis?

460. I arrived early at the restaurant last night. "Do you mind waiting for a bit?", the manager asked. "Not at all" I replied.
"Good," he said, "Take these meals to table nine."

461. I accidentally swallowed Scrabble tiles.
My next trip to the toilet could spell disaster!

How do you get a country girls attention?

A Tractor

462

What's a train's favorite number?

Two-Two!

463

What do arrogant priests have?

Altar egos.

464

For sale, barely used DeLorean.

Only driven from time to time.

465

What do you call a caveman who just wanders around?

A meanderthal.

466

In which format does a lion edit his pictures?

RAW.

467

468. What do you carve on a robot's tombstone?

Rust in peace.

469. If you rearrange the letters of postman...

he becomes very angry.

470. How many narcissists does it take to screw in a light bulb?

One. The narcissist holds the light bulb while the rest of the world revolves around him.

471. Did you hear about the cat who ate a ball of yarn?

She had mittens.

472. What do you call a disease you get in an airport?

A terminal illness.

473. Have you heard about the new restaurant called Karma?

There's no menu—you get what you deserve.

474. Why couldn't the astronaut land on the moon?

Because it was full.

475. I told my wife she drew her eyebrows too high.

She seemed surprised!

476. What do you call a bear with no teeth?

A gummy bear.

477. I ate a clock yesterday

it was so time consuming.

**478. Dad: Did you hear about the kidnapping at school?
Son: No. What happened?
Dad: The teacher woke him up.**

479. Why can't you hear a Pterodactyl go to the bathroom?

Because the P is silent!

480. The best gift I ever received for Christmas was a broken drum.

You can't beat that.

481. I would avoid the sushi if I were you.

It's a little fishy!

482. What does a mobster buried in cement soon become?

A hardened criminal.

483. Why did the graduate go to work at a knife factory?

To sharpen his skills.

484. Which Pokémon has the loudest sneeze?

Pikachu.

I told my daughter, "Go to bed, the cows are sleeping in the field." Puzzled, she asked, "What's that got to do with anything?" I chuckled, "Well, that means..."

"It's pasture bedtime!"

485

What do you call a lost wolf?

A where-wolf.

486

Wife: I'm sick of you acting like a detective, we should split up.

Me: Great idea, we can cover more ground that way!

487

A communist joke is not funny.

Unless everyone gets it.

488

I used to be addicted to soap.

But I'm clean now.

488

My buddy's foot was run over. He couldn't afford a prosthetic, so I gave him a bag of chips.

He appreciated the Fritos.

489

What do you call a guy with no shins

Tony.

490

What does a vegan have in the trunk of their car?

A spare I guess.

491

Mountains aren't just funny.

They're Hill-Areas!

492

Some people think Abraham Lincoln was a criminal.

But I know he's a cent.

493

494. What are a gas station attendant's favorite shoes?

Pumps.

495. Why did the baker sell his bread only to the rich and famous?

He wanted to work for the upper crust.

496. The guy who invented the hokey-pokey died.

They couldn't get him in the coffin. They put his right leg in, they took his right leg out...

497. What do you call an Arab who owns a dairy farm?

A milk sheikh.

498. Did you hear about the woman who tried to make a career out of being a gold digger?

It didn't really pan out.

499

What kind of language do porcupines speak?

Spine language.

500

A college professor was very worried about his recent study on earthquakes.

It turns out his findings were on shaky ground.

501

What did the cat get on the test?

A purr-fect score.

502

I have a friend who worships certain shades of blue.

He's a cyantologist.

503

How many telemarketers does it take to change a light bulb?

Only one, but he has to do it while you are eating dinner.

504 — **A brain walks into a bar and takes a seat. "I'd like some wings and a pint of beer, please," he says. "Sorry, but I can't serve you," the bartender replies.**

"You're out of your head."

505 — **Did you hear about the crustacean?**

He was accused of promoting his own shellfish interests?

506 — **I know exactly how many trees I've cut down in my lifetime.**

I keep a log.

507 — **What do you call someone who sees a robbery at an Apple Store?**

An iWitness!

508 — **I know a lot of jokes about retired people...**

but none of them work!

509

What did Adam say to his wife on the 24th of December?

It's Christmas Eve.

510

What do you call a hippie's wife?

Mississippi.

511

It hurts me to say this, but…

I have a sore throat.

512

What's a computer's favorite snack?

Microchips!

513

I signed up for this new subscription service where I receive new tires every quarter.

It's my retirement plan.

514
What is a scientist's favourite herb?
Experi-mint.

515
Where do fish go to work?
The riverbank.

516
A lion once ate an optimistic person.
But the lion couldn't keep him down.

517
Why was the limbo dancer shocked when his wallet was stolen right out of his back pocket?
Because he didn't think anyone could stoop so low.

518
I just found out Einstein is a real person!
I always thought he was a theoretical physicist.

What's on Chris Rock's Face?

Fresh Prints!

519

I had a vasectomy because I don't want kids.

To my surpprise, when I got home they were still there.

520

What do you call an alligator that owns a GPS?

A navi-gator.

521

Where do Vikings raise their babies?

In a Norsery.

522

Why did the rapper go to Whole Foods?

Because he heard they have fresh beets.

523

What do you call a wizard that sucks at football?

Fumbledore.

524

525

I made a tire joke the other day

It's finally gaining traction.

526

What do cats drink on hot summer afternoons?

Miced tea.

527

What kind of books do skunks read?

Best-smellers.

528

Where did the sheep go after high school?

Ewe-niversity.

529

Why wouldn't anybody go to the duck doctor?

They all knew he was a quack.

530

What does a Dalmatian say after eating a particularly savory bowl of dog food?

"Oh yeah, that definitely hits the spots."

531. **What do you call a chef in the special forces?**
A gravy seal.

532. **What is the opposite of a croissant?**
A happy uncle.

533. **What do you call it when Batman skips church?**
Christian Bail.

534. **Have you heard about those new corduroy pillows?**
They're making headlines.

535. **Did you hear about the Italian chef who died**
He pasta way!

536. **Finally, my winter fat has gone.**
Now, I have spring rolls.

537 I heard jokes about brooms are becoming really popular.
They're sweeping the nation.

538 I came home from work yesterday to find someone had stolen all my lamps.
I was delighted!

539 What is a shark's favorite game?
Swallow the leader.

540 "I'm sorry," and "I apologize," are the same statement.
Except at funerals.

541 What does the wifi router wear while exercising?
A broadband.

542

I have been told that I have a dad bod.

I like to think I am a father figure.

543

I lost my job as a masseuse.

I guess I rub people the wrong way.

544

What's the main cause of dry skin?

A towel.

545

The numbers 19 and 20 got into a fight.

21

546

What do astronauts carry their lunch in?

A launch box.

547
If you're being chased by a serial killer,
you're both running for your life.

548
Did you hear about the two mind readers who met on the street?
The first one said, "Well, you're fine. How am I?"

549
How come Peter Pan is always flying?
He never lands.

550
When my daughter was born, the nurse brought in a heated blanket.
I asked if it was womb temperature.

551
My friend was a struggling artist until he decided to just do sculptures.
He made over six figures last year.

552. Why did the bald man paint rabbits on his head?

Because from a distance they looked like hares.

553. Why did the coffee go to the police?

It got mugged.

554. Why did the bird make fun of everyone?

It was a mockingbird!

555. Why was Sea World closed?

For training porpoises.

556. Why can't you trust atoms?

Because they make up everything.

557. There I was this morning, sitting and drinking my coffee in my slippers.

When I thought to myself, I really need to clean some mugs.

558
Did you hear NASA found another planet?
It's out of this world.

559
What was the man feeling after he got swindled right under Big Ben?
He was ticked off.

560
What do you get from a pampered cow?
Spoiled milk.

561
How does a mouse feel after it takes a bath?
Squeaky clean.

562
My kid wants to invent a pencil with an eraser on each end,
but I just don't see the point.

563
Why is there so much peace between farmers?
Because they are part of agreeCULTURE.

564

Why did the Mayan take Xanax?

To prevent hispanic attacks.

565

My wife divorced me because she got sick of me using Greek letters in everything.

She wouldn't believe I could Δ

566

Diarrhea isn't your fault;

it runs in your jeans.

567

My wife started our daughter's potty training. To show support, I left a note saying,

"you can do do this"

568

Why did the chicken cross the playground?

To get to the other slide.

What did the sheep say to his fiancée?

"There's something I have to tell you: I love ewe."

569

I sent my hearing aids out for repair three weeks ago.

I haven't heard anything since!

570

Why did the pregnant woman race to the hospital?

She wanted to have a speedy delivery.

571

What happened when the elephant sat on the grape?

It let out a little whine.

572

I read that by law you must turn on your headlights when it's raining in Sweden.

But how am I supposed to know when it is raining in Sweden?

573

574. When is a boat wearable?
When it's cap-sized.

575. What do you call two monkeys who share an Amazon account?
Prime mates.

576. Why are bakers so rich?
They make so much dough.

577. Thinking of having my ashes stored in a glass urn.
Remains to be seen.

578. What language do people speak in the middle of the earth?
Core-ean.

579. I can't find my 'Gone in 60 seconds' DVD.
It was here a minute ago.

Why can't a leopard hide?

Because he's always spotted.

580

What do bees do when they move to a new hive?

They throw a house swarming party.

581

What do you call two people who bond over clothing?

Vest Friends!

582

Why is grass so dangerous?

Because it's full of blades.

583

You know, people say they pick their nose,

but I feel like I was just born with mine.

584

How do you make holy water

You boil the hell out of it.

585

586

Did you hear they arrested the devil?

Yeah, they got him on possession.

587

Police arrested a bottle of water because it was wanted in three different states:

solid, liquid, and gas.

588

What do you call a pig after it exits the voting booth?

Polled pork.

589

Why do vampires seem sick?

They're always coffin.

590

At the job interview, they asked me, "Where do you see yourself in five years?"

I told him, "I think we'll still be using mirrors in five years."

591. What happens when it rains cats and dogs?
You have to be careful not to step in a poodle.

592. Why did the stadium get so hot after the game?
Because all the fans left.

593. What do you call it when Dwayne Johnson buys a cutting tool?
Rock pay-for scissors.

594. Not to brag but I made six figures last year.
I was also named worst employee at the toy factory.

595. What do you call a sad cup of coffee?
Depresso.

596. Why did the masseuse have to close up his shop?
He kept rubbing people the wrong way.

597

A man is begging a judge to let him off jury duty because of his job. "I'm sure your company can get along fine without you for a few days," the judge tells the man.

"I know," the man answers. "But that's what I'm trying to prevent them from figuring out."

598

What do you call a group of babies

An infantry!

599

I did not use to believe in Chiropractors.

But now I stand corrected.

600

I just invented a thought-controlled air freshener.

It makes scents if you think about it.

601

What's a bad wizard's favorite computer program?

Spell-check.

602 What do you get when you cross a CD player with a secretary?

A stereotype.

603 What has four wheels and flies?

A garbage truck!

604 What did the couch say halfway through the marathon?

"Sofa, so good."

605 What do you call two octopuses that look the same?

Itenticle.

606 I went to a seafood disco last week!

Pulled a mussel!

607 I wondered why the Frisbee was getting bigger.

Then it hit me.

608

What do you call Batman when he's hurt?

Bruised Wayne.

609

Found out my wife is cheating on me today. When I asked when she'd be home she said "10-15 minutes max"

My name is Nathan.

610

What do you call a zombie who cooks stir fries?

Dead man wok-ing.

611

I asked the librarian if books about paranoia were available.

She looked up and whispered, "They're right behind you".

612

I used to work in a shoe-recycling shop.

It was sole crushing!

613
I'm reading a book about anti-gravity.

It's impossible to put down.

614
There are 10 kinds of people in this world.

Those that understand binary code and those that do not.

615
What do Santa's elves listen to ask they work?

Wrap music!

616
What do you call a monster with high IQ?

FrankEinstein.

617
How do you kill a circus?

Go for the juggler.

618
Why did the sticker need a lawyer?

It was ripped off.

619. What do you call it when someone crashes into a police officer?

A run-in with the law!

620. Why are elephants banned from public swimming pools?

They always drop their trunks.

621. What happened to the robber who stole the lamp?

Oh, he got a very light sentence.

622. My daughter thinks I don't respect her privacy

At least that's what she wrote in her diary.

623. What do you call a zombie's butt?

Deadass

624. I lost 3 fingers on my right hand, so I asked my doctor if I would still be able to write with it.

She said "maybe but I wouldn't count on it".

625. **A couple of cups of yogurt walk into a country club. "We don't serve your kind here," the bartender says. "Why not?" one yogurt asks.**

"We're cultured."

626. **Can February March?**

No, but April May!

627. **How do vampires start letters?**

Tomb it may concern.

628. **What rock group has four men that don't sing?**

Mount Rushmore.

629. **Why does Dracula always bite people in the neck?**

Because he's a neck-romancer.

630

Why didn't the priest read the T&Cs?

Because the devil's in the details!

631

Why were all the mice in disguise?

They were attending a mouse-querade party.

632

Why didn't the turkey finish his dinner?

He was already stuffed.

633

What do you call a man who owes money?

Bill.

634

Why did the Beatles break up?

They started to bug each other.

635

What kind of car does Luke Skywalker drive?

A To-yoda.

What's Moby Dick's favorite dinner?

Fish 'n' ships.

636

My wife asked me if I wanted to come to yoga.

I replied, "Namaste home."

637

I saw a couple arguing at the gym today.

They weren't working out.

638

Singing in the shower is fun until you get soap in your mouth.

Because then it's a soap opera.

639

This weekend, the Geriatric Cheerleaders of America broke the world record for the largest number of men stacked on top of each other.

It was a great pyramid of geezers.

640

641
Just paid $200 for a belt that doesn't fit!

What a huge waist!

642
Did you hear about the duck that went to rehab?

He was addicted to quack.

643
I'm starting a new dating service in Prague.

It's called Czech-Mate.

644
Why do Dads take an extra pair of socks when they go golfing?

In case they get a hole in one.

645
Why did the raisin go out with the prune?

Because he couldn't find a date.

646
What's the best thing about Switzerland?

I don't know, but the flag is a big plus.

647

What do diplomats say on Halloween?

"Trick or treaty."

648

I found a vampire in my freezer.

Dracooler.

649

What kind of monster loves to dance?

The boogieman.

650

What's blue and tastes like red paint?

Blue paint.

651

I was texting my daughter to see if she wanted to eat at a certain restaurant. She replied "Meet there?"

I said "Yes, veggies too!"

652 — **I got a hen to regularly count her own eggs.**
She's a real mathamachicken!

653 — **I quit my job as a mailman when they gave me my first letter to deliver.**
I looked at it and thought, "This isn't for me."

654 — **Waiter, there is a slug in my salad!**
I'm sorry sir, I didn't realize you were a vegetarian!

655 — **My dog hasn't been doing so great today**
I asked him "how's your day?" and all he said was "ruff."

656 — **What do you get when you cross a sheep with a kung fu master?**
Lamb chops.

657 — **What has two legs and flies?**
A pair of trousers.

What do you call two weed dispensaries merging?

A *joint* venture.

658

Did you hear about the serial killer who was targeting medical examiners?

They were able to catch him easily.
He was cutting coroners.

659

Why was the chicken team so bad at baseball?

They kept hitting fowl balls.

660

Why do plants hate math?

It gives them square roots.

661

One day, a flying saucer lands in Times Square and tries to park in the middle of the sidewalk. Immediately a traffic cop rushes over to the Martian and says, "You can't park that thing here. Go find a legal spot." The Martian looks up and says, "Take me to your meter."

662

663. What do you say to your sister when she's crying?
Are you having a Crisis?

664. I named my printer Bob Marley.
Because it's always jammin'.

665. I don't trust those trees.
They seem kind of shady.

666. I wasn't expecting to be diagnosed as color blind.
It really came out of the purple.

667. I saw a 1000-year-old oil stain.
It was from ancient Greece.

668. You should never lie to an X-Ray tech.
They can see right through you.

669 **I'm desperately trying to find out who's been pooping on my lawn.**
It's a real who dung it.

670 **What's the least spoken language in the world?**
Sign language

671 **Why do oceans never go out of style?**
They're always current.

672 **I think you'll like this joke, even though it's a little long.**
long.

673 **I told my doctor I heard buzzing.**
But he said it's just a bug going around.

674 **What did the sun say when it was introduced to the earth?**
"Pleased to heat you."

675. Why are shooting stars so fast?

They're traveling light.

676. What did the astronaut think of the takeoff?

She thought it was a blast.

677. What did the rope say after it tangled?

"Oh no, knot again!"

678. Why is Homer Simpson bad at singing scales?

He always gets stuck at "Doh!"

679. How did the robber get caught at the art gallery?

He was framed.

680. How did the scientist invent bug spray?

She started from scratch.

681

My dog swallowed a whole bag of Scrabble tiles. We took him to the vet to get him checked out.

No word yet.

682

How can you tell when a fairy has been using your computer?

Pixel dust.

683

I normally grill my bacon.

But now I'm running out of questions to ask it.

684

Did you hear about the ATM that got addicted to money?

It suffered from withdrawals.

685

I passed all of my courses except for Greek Mythology.

That has always been my Achilles' elbow.

686. People are usually shocked that I have a Police record.

But I love their greatest hits!

687. What happens when you throw a clock in the air?

Time's up!

688. Why did the paranoid fencer only use a sabre?

He had thrust issues.

689. I struggle with Roman Numerals until I get to 159.

Then it just CLIX.

690. Where did the cat go after losing its tail?

To the retail store.

691. What do you call an angry carrot?

A steamed veggie.

692
My doctor told me I'm going deaf.
The news was hard for me to hear.

693
Why do vampires have no friends?
They suck.

694
Why are spiders so smart?
They can find everything on the web.

695
How many symbols do you need to type on a keyboard to make a heart?
Less than three.

696
What did the mermaid wear to math class?
Algae-bra.

697
What do you call a million rabbits walking backwards?
A receding hareline!

698

At the doctor's office, Tom was getting a check up. "I have good news and bad news," says the doctor. "The good news is you have 24 hours left to live." Tom replies, "That's the good news?!" Then the doctor says, "The bad news is I should have told you that yesterday."

699

A construction worker accidentally cuts off one of his ears with an electric saw. He calls out to a guy walking on the street below, "Hey, do you see my ear down there?" The guy on the street picks up an ear. "Is this it?" "No," replies the construction worker, "mine had a pencil behind it."

700

A man calls his lawyer and asks: "How much would you charge me to answer three questions" The lawyer replies: "Four hundred dollars." The man retorts: "That's a bit steep don t you think?"

And the lawyer replies: "I suppose so. What's you third question?"

701

A little old lady was speeding down the road while knitting. A cop caught up to her and, driving alongside her, shouted, "Pull over!"

"No," the little old lady replied. "They're mittens."

703

What's a monster's favorite snack?

Ghoul scout cookies.

704

What do you get when you cross a comedian with crochet.

A knit wit.

705

Never challenge Death to a pillow fight.

You can't handle the reaper cushions.

706

My wife said she'd leave me if I kept making Star Wars jokes.

I said "May divorce be with you."

707

My wife was stopped by the cops tonight. They thought she might have been drink driving. The cop asked her to say the alphabet starting with the letter M.

She said "Malphabet."

708

A farmer was counting his cows and got to 196.

But when he rounded them up, they were 200.

709

Why can't pirates ever finish the alphabet?

They always get lost at C.

710

What's a horse's number one priority when voting?

The stable economy!

711

My wife said if I bought her a stupid gift this Christmas, she would burn it.

So I bought her a candle.

712

Amber Heard confessed to having a child with Charlie Sheen. The child went to live with his father and took his name.

Both parents agreed the child should be sheen and not heard.

713

What do Jesus, Columbus, Washington, Lincoln, and MLK have in common?

They were all born on holidays.

714

What did the two pieces of bread say on their wedding day.

It was loaf at first sight.

715

Whoever stole my copy of Microsoft Office, I will find you!

You have my Word!

716

Why did the bullet end up losing his job?

He got fired.

717. On his deathbed, a lifelong Republican told his best friend that he was switching parties and becoming a Democrat. "My God," his friend replied, "why would you do such a thing?" "Simple," the man muttered in his last breath, "because I'd rather one of them die than one of us."

718. Why haven't aliens visited our Solar System yet?

They looked at the reviews, only 1 star!

719. What group of people never get angry?

Nomads.

720. Why did Eminem prefer the Johnson & Johnson vaccine?

You only get one shot.

721. Why did the police investigate the seafood restaurant?

They knew something fishy was going on.

How did the astronaut feel when he ran into the alien with six lasers for arms?

Stunned.

(722)

Where do hair colorists sit when they go to baseball games?

In the bleachers.

(723)

How did the pirate get his ship so cheap?

It was on sail.

(724)

How long does a jousting tournament last?

Until knightfall.

(725)

I used to be addicted to the hokey pokey.

But I turned myself around.

(726)

727

A father and his small son were standing in front of the tiger's cage at the zoo. The father was explaining how ferocious and strong tigers are, and the boy was taking it all in with a serious expression. "Dad," the boy said finally, "if the tiger got out of his cage and ate you up…" "Yes, son?" the father said expectantly. And the boy finished: "What bus should I take home?"

728

The military is considering bringing in emotional support dogs for people deployed on extended submarine tours.

They think installing subwoofers will be good for morale.

729

If Snoop Dogg were an actual dog, what breed would he be?

Doperman.

730

**Interviewer: Can you explain these 4 jobless years in your resume?
Applicant: That's when I went to Yale.**

Interviewer: Impressive! You are hired!
Applicant: Thanks, I really need this yob.

731. I love going outdoors. It is so much easier than going outwindows.

732. My wife changed after she became a vegetarian.
It's like I've never seen herbivore.

733. My friend quit his job at BMW.
He gave no indication he was leaving.

734. Did you hear about the phlebotomist that had to quit her job?
She said her work was all in vein.

735. Someone just called my phone, sneezed, and then just hung up.
I am getting sick and tired of all these cold calls.

736. I'm afraid of speed bumps
But I'm slowly getting over it

737

A wealthy Frenchman was showing off his yachts. "This is un, this is deux, this is trois, this is quatre, this is six..." "What happened to five?" his wife asked.

"Cinq" he answered.

739

My wife said she'd break up with me if I kept making puns about our seasonings and spices.

I guess it's only a matter of thyme until bay leaves.

740

Why was Pavlov's hair so messy?

He didn't condition it.

741

My wife told me that my salads are a bit on the dry side...

It's something that needs addressing.

742

What is the loudest color?

YELLow

743

Did you hear about the T-Rex that sells guns?

He's a small arms dealer.

744

What did the pine trees wear to the lake?

swimming trunks.

745

What do you call Father Christmas in an orange suit?

Fanta Claus.

746

What do you get when you cross a doctor and a lemon?

Lemon-aid.

747

How do you make a hobbit?

You frodocopy it!

748

What's the creepiest pokemon?

Peek at you.

If you tell a joke to Tommy and at first, he doesn't get it, don't worry.

Hilfiger it out.

749

What do clouds wear?

Thunder wear.

750

What do you call a sheep farm with only rams?

Ewes-less.

751

I had a couple coins in my wallet, so I donated it to global warming research.

It's climate change.

752

I invented a new word today.

Plagiarism.

753

My wife said, "You really have no sense of direction, do you?"

I said, "Where did that come from?"

754

I showed my Mexican friends I know a little Spanish by saying "mucho" and they seemed really flattered.

They said it meant a lot to them.

756

My wife texted me "I love u"

I said that's my favorite letter too.

757

I went into a toy store to do some early Christmas shopping and asked the assistant, "Where are the Schwarzenegger dolls?"

He said, "Aisle B, back."

758

What do you call a man in debt?

Owen.

759

My wife begged me to stop telling Scandinavian puns.

I told her, "Fine, I'm Finnished."

760

EXCLUSIVE FREE GOODIES!

We hope you've enjoyed every chuckle and snicker this Dad Jokes book has to offer! And while the jokes may have reached their punchline, the fun continues. As a thank you, we're including two bonus printable books: a Themed Word Search puzzle book for a delightful brain exercise, and a Sudoku book to keep your mind sharp and engaged. Claim your free copies by scanning the QR code below and enjoy more entertaining moments on us!

Scan Me

serene-square.ck.page/bonus

SERENE SQUARE PUBLISHING

Printed in Great Britain
by Amazon